SNAP REVISION GEOMETRY AND MEASURES

SNAP REVISION

GEOMETRY AND MEASURES

(for papers 1, 2 and 3)

AQA GCSE Maths Higher

AQA GCSE MATHS HIGHER

REVISE TRICKY TOPICS IN A SNAP

Maths Contents

	Revise	Practise	Review
Angles and Shapes 1	p. 4	p. 8	p. 18
Angles and Shapes 2	p. 6	p. 8	p. 18
Transformations	p. 10	p. 19	p. 28
Constructions	p. 12	p. 19	p. 28
Area and Volume 1	p. 14	p. 21	p. 30
Area and Volume 2	p. 16	p. 21	p. 30
Congruence and Geometrical Problems	p. 22	p. 31	p. 38
Right-Angled Triangles	p. 24	p. 32	p. 39
Sine and Cosine Rules	p. 26	p. 33	p. 40
Circles	p. 34	p. 41	p. 42
Vectors	p. 36	p. 41	p. 42
Answers	p. 43		

Published by Collins
An imprint of HarperCollins*Publishers*
1 London Bridge Street,
London, SE1 9GF

© HarperCollins*Publishers* Limited 2017

9780008242367

First published 2017

10 9 8 7 6 5 4 3 2 1

British Library Cataloguing in Publication Data.

A CIP record of this book is available from the British Library.

Printed in Great Britain by Bell and Bain Ltd, Glasgow.

ACKNOWLEDGEMENTS

The author and publisher are grateful to the copyright holders for permission to use quoted materials and images.

All images are © Shutterstock.com

Every effort has been made to trace copyright holders and obtain their permission for the use of copyright material. The author and publisher will gladly receive information enabling them to rectify any error or omission in subsequent editions. All facts are correct at time of going to press.

How To Use This Book

To get the most out of this revision guide, just work your way through the book in the order it is presented.

This is how it works:

Revise

Clear and concise revision notes help you get to grips with the topic

Revise

Key Points and Key Words explain the important information you need to know

Revise

A Quick Test at the end of every topic is a great way to check your understanding

Practise

Practice questions for each topic reinforce the revision content you have covered

Review

The Review section is a chance to revisit the topic to improve your recall in the exam

Angles and Shapes 1

You must be able to:

- Recognise relationships between angles
- Use the properties of angles to work out unknown angles
- Recognise different types of triangle
- Understand and use the properties of special types of quadrilaterals.

Angle Facts

- There are three types of angle:
  - acute: less than 90°
  - obtuse: between 90° and 180°
  - reflex: between 180° and 360°.
- Angles on a straight line add up to 180°.
- Angles around a point add up to 360°.
- Vertically opposite angles are equal.

Angles in Parallel Lines

- Parallel lines never meet. The lines are always the same distance apart.
- Alternate angles are equal.
- Corresponding angles are equal.
- Co-interior or allied angles add up to 180°.

Work out the sizes of angles a, b, c and d.
Give reasons for your answers.

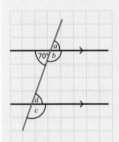

$a = 70°$ (vertically opposite angles are equal)

$b = 110°$ (angles on a straight line add up to 180°, so $b = 180° - 70°$)

$c = 110°$ (corresponding to b; corresponding angles are equal)

$d = 70°$ (corresponding to a; corresponding angles are equal)

Triangles

- Angles in a triangle add up to 180°.
- There are several types of triangle:
  - equilateral: three equal sides and three equal angles of 60°
  - isosceles: two equal sides and two equal angles (opposite the equal sides)
  - scalene: no sides or angles are equal
  - right-angled: one 90° angle.

Alternate Angles

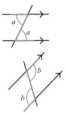

Corresponding Angles

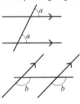

Allied Angles

$c + d = 180°$

> **Key Point**
>
> Examiners will **not** accept terms like 'Z angles' or 'F angles'. Always use correct terminology when giving reasons.

ABC is an isosceles triangle and HE is parallel to GD. BAF is a straight line. Angle $FAE = 81°$

Calculate **a)** angle ABC and **b)** angle ACB.

Give reasons for your answers.

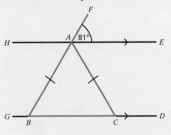

a) Angle $HAB = 81°$ (vertically opposite FAE), so angle $ABC = 81°$ (alternate angle to HAB)

b) Angle $ACB = 81°$ (angle ABC = angle ACB; base angles of an isosceles triangle are equal.)

> There are several different ways of solving this question.

Special Quadrilaterals

- The interior angles in a quadrilateral add up to 360°.
- You need to know the properties of these special quadrilaterals:

	Sides	Angles	Lines of Symmetry	Rotational Symmetry	Diagonals
parallelogram	opposite sides are equal and parallel	diagonally opposite angles are equal	none	order 2	diagonals bisect each other
rhombus	all sides are equal and opposite sides are parallel	opposite angles are equal	two	order 2	diagonals bisect each other at 90°
kite	two pairs of adjacent sides are equal	one pair of opposite angles is equal	one	none	diagonals cross at 90°
trapezium	one pair of opposite sides is parallel		none (an isosceles trapezium has one)	none	

Angles and Shapes 2

You must be able to:

- Work out angles in a polygon
- Answer questions on regular polygons
- Understand and use bearings.

Geometry and Measures

Angles in a Polygon

- A **polygon** is a closed shape with at least three straight sides.
- **Regular** polygons are shapes where all the sides and angles are equal.
- **Irregular** polygons are shapes where some or all of the sides and angles are different.
- For all polygons:
  - at any **vertex** (corner): **interior** angle + **exterior** angle = 180°
  - sum of all exterior angles = 360°
- To work out the sum of the interior angles in a polygon, you can split it into triangles from one vertex.
- For example, a pentagon is divided into three triangles, so the sum of the interior angles is 3 × 180° = 540°
- The sum of the interior angles for any polygon can be calculated using the formula:

 Sum of Interior Angles = $(n - 2) \times 180°$
where n = number of sides

Work out the sum of the interior angles of a decagon (10 sides).

Sum = $(10 - 2) \times 180°$ ⟵ Use the formula: Sum = $(n - 2) \times 180°$
   = $8 \times 180°$
   = $1440°$

Regular Polygons

- In regular polygons:

 Number of Sides (n) × Exterior Angle = 360°
So, Exterior Angle = $360° \div n$

Work out the size of the interior angles in a regular hexagon (6 sides).

Exterior angle   = $360° \div 6 = 60°$ ⟵ Use the formula: Exterior Angle = $360° \div n$
Interior angle + 60° = $180°$ ⟵
Interior angle   = $180° - 60°$ Interior Angle + Exterior Angle = 180°
                    = $120°$

Pentagon

Exterior Angles

Interior Angles

A regular polygon has an interior angle of 156°.

Work out the number of sides that the polygon has.

Exterior angle = 180° – interior angle
= 180° – 156°
= 24°

Number of sides = 360° ÷ 24°
= 15

Scale Drawings and Bearings

- **Bearings** are always measured in a clockwise direction from north (000°).
- Bearings always have three figures.

A ship sails from Mevagissey on a bearing of 130° for 22km.

a) Draw an accurate diagram to show this information and state the scale you have used.

b) What bearing would take the ship back to the harbour?

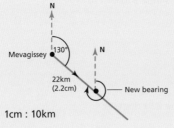

1cm : 10km

New bearing to return to harbour = 310° ◄—————— Measure with a protractor.

Key Point

Always place the 0 to 180 line of the protractor onto the north-south line.

Quick Test

1. For a regular icosagon (20 sides), work out a) the sum of the interior angles and b) the size of one interior angle.
2. A regular polygon has an interior angle of 150°.
   How many sides does the polygon have?
3. Two yachts leave port at the same time.
   Yacht A sails on a bearing of 040° for 35km.
   Yacht B sails on a bearing of 120° for 60km.
   Using a scale of 1cm : 10km, draw the route taken by both yachts.
   What is the bearing of yacht B from yacht A?

Key Words

polygon
regular
irregular
vertex
interior
exterior
bearing

Practice Questions

Angles and Shapes 1 & 2

1 Work out the size of angles j, k, l and m, giving a reason for each answer.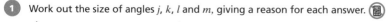

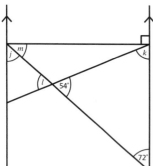

[4]

2 $ABCD$ is a parallelogram.
AB is parallel to CD and AD is parallel to BC. Angle $BAD = 110°$

Work out:

a) Angle DCB. [1]

b) Angle ABC. [1]

3 The angles in a quadrilateral are x, 2.5x, 3x and 2.5x degrees.

Calculate the size of the largest angle. [2]

4 Work out the interior angle of a regular decagon. [2]

5 A and B are two points.

If the bearing of B from A is 036°, what is the bearing of A from B? [1]

6 A regular polygon has an exterior angle of 45°.

a) Work out how many sides the polygon has. [1]

b) What is the name of the polygon? [1]

Total Marks _____ / 13

Angles and Shapes 1 & 2

1 Work out the value of x.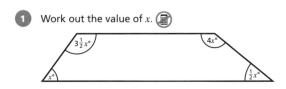

Answer _____ [2]

2 The interior angle of a regular polygon is 150°.

Work out how many sides the polygon has. 🖩

Answer _____ [2]

3 A helicopter leaves its base and flies 40km on a bearing of 050° and then 30km on a bearing of 105°. 🖩

a) Draw a scale diagram to show this information. How far is the helicopter from its base?

Answer _____ [2]

b) On what bearing does the helicopter need to fly in order to return to its base?

Answer _____ [1]

Total Marks _____ / 7

Transformations

You must be able to:

- Identify, describe and construct transformations of shapes, including reflections, rotations, translations and enlargements
- Describe the changes achieved by combinations of transformations.

Transformations

- **Reflection:**
  - Each point on the image is the same distance from the mirror line as the corresponding point on the object
  - The object and the image are **congruent** (same size and shape)
  - To define a reflection on a coordinate grid, the equation of the mirror line should be stated.
- **Rotation** is described by stating the:
  - Direction rotated (clockwise or anticlockwise)
  - Angle of rotation (which is usually a multiple of 90° in the exam)
  - Centre of rotation (point about which the shape is rotated).

> **Key Point**
>
> There is no need to state clockwise or anticlockwise for a rotation of 180°.

a) Describe the transformation that maps triangle ABC onto triangle $A'B'C'$.

The transformation that maps ABC to $A'B'C'$ is a rotation of 90° anticlockwise (or 270° clockwise) about the origin (0, 0).

b) Describe the transformation that maps triangle $A'B'C'$ onto triangle $A''B''C''$.

The transformation that maps $A'B'C'$ to $A''B''C''$ is a rotation of 180° about the origin (0, 0).

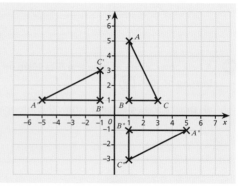

- **Translation:**
  - The shape does not rotate – it moves left or right and up or down – and stays the same size
  - The translation is represented by a **column vector** $\begin{pmatrix} x \\ y \end{pmatrix}$

> **Key Point**
>
> x represents the distance moved **horizontally**: **positive** means to the **right** and **negative** means to the **left**.
>
> y represents the distance moved **vertically**: **positive** means **up** and **negative** means **down**.

Describe the transformation that takes shape A to shape B.

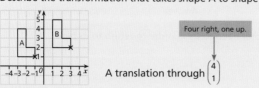

Four right, one up.

A translation through $\begin{pmatrix} 4 \\ 1 \end{pmatrix}$

- Enlargement:
  - The shape of the object is not changed, only its size. The enlarged shape is similar to the original shape
  - The scale factor determines whether the object gets bigger (scale factor > 1) or smaller (scale factor < 1)
  - Scale factors can be negative. This results in:
    - A 180° rotation of the object
    - The image being on the opposite side of the centre of enlargement to the object
  - When describing the enlargement, state the scale factor and the centre of enlargement.

Key Point

Scale factors that result in the object getting smaller are often represented as a fraction.

Enlarge triangle A by scale factor 2, centre of enlargement (1, 2). Label the transformed triangle B.

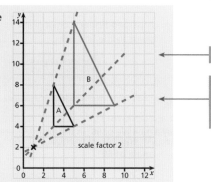

All construction lines must remain.

The side lengths of triangle B are twice the length of the corresponding sides of triangle A. However, the area of triangle B is four times bigger.

scale factor 2

Combinations of Transformations

- It is possible for two or more transformations to be applied to a shape, one after the other.

Enlarge triangle C by scale factor $-\frac{1}{2}$ about centre of enlargement (0, 0) to form triangle D.

Transform triangle D by a reflection in the line $y = 1$ to form triangle E.

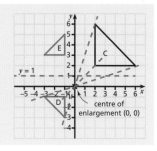

centre of enlargement (0, 0)

Key Words

reflection
congruent
rotation
translation
column vector
enlargement
similar
scale factor

Quick Test

1. Describe the single transformation that takes:
   a) triangle A to triangle B
   b) triangle A to triangle C
   c) triangle A to triangle D.

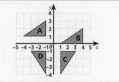

Constructions

You must be able to:

- Use a ruler and a pair of compasses to produce different constructions, including bisectors
- Describe a locus and solve problems involving loci
- Understand and construct plans and elevations of 3D shapes.

Constructions

- The perpendicular bisector of line AB. 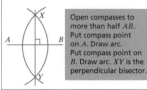 Open compasses to more than half AB. Put compass point on A. Draw arc. Put compass point on B. Draw arc. XY is the perpendicular bisector.	- A **perpendicular** from a given point to the line AB. Put compass point on C. Draw arc. Keep radius the same. Put compass point on E. Draw arc. Put compass point on D. Draw arc. Join C to the point where the arcs cross.
- An **angle bisector**. 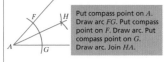 Put compass point on A. Draw arc FG. Put compass point on F. Draw arc. Put compass point on G. Draw arc. Join HA.	- An **equilateral triangle** and an **angle of 60°**. Open compasses to length AB. Put point on A. Draw arc. Put compass point on B. Draw arc. Join AJ and BJ. Angle $A = 60°$

> **Key Point**
>
> The perpendicular distance from a point to a line is the shortest distance to the line.

> **Key Point**
>
> To construct a perpendicular at a given point on a line:
>
> Put the compass point on that point.
>
> Draw two arcs on the line either side of that point.
>
> Then construct the perpendicular bisector of the two new points.

Defining a Locus

- A locus is the path taken by a point that is obeying certain rules.
- The plural of locus is loci.

- The locus of points that are a **fixed distance from a given point** A is a circle. 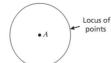 Locus of points	- The locus of points that are a **fixed distance from a line** AB.  Locus of points
- The locus of points that are the **same distance from two lines** AB and AC. This is the angle bisector. 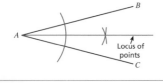 Locus of points	- The locus of points that are equidistant, or the **same distance**, from two points A and B. This is the perpendicular bisector. Locus of points

Loci Problems

A guard dog is tied to a post by a 4-metre long rope.

Accurately draw the locus of the points the dog can reach using a scale of 1cm : 1m

The solution would be a shaded circle of radius 4cm.
The dog could reach the circumference of the circle and all points within it.

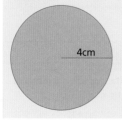

4cm   Not Drawn Accurately

Plans and Elevations

- The plan view of a 3D shape shows what it looks like from above – a bird's eye view.
- The side elevation is the view of a 3D shape from the side.
- The front elevation is the view from the front.

Here is a 3D shape made from centimetre cubes drawn on isometric paper.

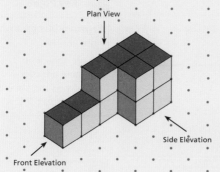

Plan View

Side Elevation

Front Elevation

On squared paper, draw:
a) the plan view

b) the front elevation

c) the side elevation.

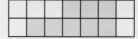

Quick Test

1. Describe how you would accurately construct an angle of 30°.
2. A rectangular vegetable plot $ABCD$ measures 6m by 3m.
   A goat is tethered at corner A by a 4m rope.
   Accurately draw the plot and construct the locus of the points that the goat can reach. Scale 1cm : 1m. Shade the region of the vegetable plot that can be eaten by the goat.

Key Words

perpendicular
   bisector
locus / loci
equidistant
plan view
elevation

Area and Volume 1

You must be able to:

- Recall and use the formulae for the circumference and area of a circle
- Recall and use the formula for the area of a trapezium
- Recall and use the formulae for the volume and surface area of a prism
- Recall and use the formulae for the volume and surface area of a cylinder.

Circles

LEARN

Circumference of a Circle $(C) = 2\pi r$ or $C = \pi d$

Area of a Circle $(A) = \pi r^2$

Key Point

The symbol π represents the number **pi**.

π can be approximated to 3.14 or $\frac{22}{7}$

Work out the circumference and area of a circle with radius 9cm. Give your answers to 1 decimal place.

Circumference

$C = 2 \times \pi \times 9$

$\quad = 18 \times \pi$

$\quad = 56.5$cm (to 1 d.p.)

Area

$A = \pi \times 9^2$

$\quad = \pi \times 81$

$\quad = 254.5$cm² (to 1 d.p.)

Trapeziums

LEARN

The area of a **trapezium** is:

$$A = \tfrac{1}{2}(a + b)h$$

where a and b are the **parallel** sides and h is the **perpendicular** height

Key Point

Perpendicular means 'at right angles'.

Parallel means 'in the same direction and always the same distance apart'.

- This formula can be proved:

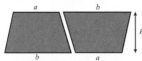

- Two identical trapeziums fit together to make a parallelogram with base $a + b$ and height h.
- The area of the parallelogram is $(a + b)h$.
- Therefore, the area of each trapezium is $\tfrac{1}{2}(a + b)h$.

Key Point

The area of a parallelogram is: $A = bh$

Work out the area of the trapezium.

$A = \tfrac{1}{2} \times (5 + 10) \times 4$

$\quad = 30$cm²

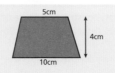

Prisms

- A right prism is a 3D shape that has the same **cross-section** running all the way through it.

 Volume of a Prism = Area of Cross-Section × Length

- The surface area is the sum of the areas of all the **faces**.

Work out the volume and surface area of the triangular prism.

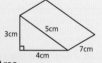

Volume
Area of the cross-section
$= \frac{1}{2} \times 3 \times 4 = 6\text{cm}^2$
Volume $= 6 \times 7$
$= 42\text{cm}^3$

Surface Area
Five faces:
Two triangular faces = 6 + 6 = 12
Base = 4 × 7 = 28
Side = 3 × 7 = 21
Slanted side = 5 × 7 = 35
Total surface area:
12 + 28 + 21 + 35 = 96cm²

Cylinders

 Volume of a Cylinder = $\pi r^2 h$

Surface Area of a Cylinder = $2\pi r h + 2\pi r^2$

Work out the volume and surface area of the cylinder. Give your answers in terms of π.

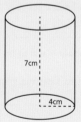

Volume
$V = \pi \times 4^2 \times 7$
$= 112\pi\text{cm}^3$

Surface Area
$SA = 2 \times \pi \times 4 \times 7 + 2 \times \pi \times 4^2$
$= 56\pi + 32\pi$
$= 88\pi\text{cm}^2$

Key Point

A cylinder is just like any other right prism. To find the volume, you multiply the area of the cross-section (circular face) by the length of the cylinder.

Quick Test

1. Calculate the volume and surface area of a cylinder with radius 4cm and height 6cm.
2. Work out the area of the trapezium.

3. Calculate the circumference and area of a circle, diameter 7cm.

Key Words

trapezium
parallel
perpendicular
cross-section
face

Area and Volume 2

You must be able to:

- Find the volume of a pyramid
- Find the volume and surface area of a cone
- Find the volume of a frustum
- Find the volume and surface area of a sphere
- Find the area and volume of composite shapes.

Pyramids

- A **pyramid** is a 3D shape in which lines drawn from the **vertices** of the base meet at a point.

 LEARN

Volume of a Pyramid $= \frac{1}{3} \times$ Area of the Base $\times$ Height

> **Key Point**
>
> A pyramid is usually defined by the base, e.g. a square-based pyramid or a triangular-based pyramid.

Work out the volume of the square-based pyramid.

$V = \frac{1}{3} \times 9 \times 9 \times 7$

$= 189 \text{cm}^3$

Cones

- A **cone** is a 3D shape with a circular base that tapers to a single vertex.

 LEARN

Volume of a Cone $= \frac{1}{3} \pi r^2 h$

Surface Area of a Cone $= \pi r l + \pi r^2$

Work out **a)** the volume and **b)** the surface area of the cone.
Give your answers to 1 decimal place.

a) $h = \sqrt{6^2 - 4^2}$ ← First find the height using Pythagoras' Theorem.

$h = \sqrt{20}$

$V = \frac{1}{3} \times \pi \times 4^2 \times \sqrt{20} = 74.9 \text{cm}^3$

b) $SA = (\pi \times 4 \times 6) + (\pi \times 4^2) = 125.7 \text{cm}^2$

- A **frustum** is the 3D shape that remains when a cone is cut parallel to its base and the top cone removed.
- The original cone and the smaller cone that is removed are always similar.

 LEARN

$$\text{Volume of a Frustum} = \text{Volume of Whole Cone} - \text{Volume of Top Cone}$$

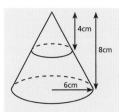

Calculate the volume of the frustum. Leave your answer in terms of π.

Radius of small cone = 3cm

The two cones are similar with scale factor 2.

$$V = \frac{1}{3}\left(\pi \times 6^2 \times 8\right) - \frac{1}{3}\left(\pi \times 3^2 \times 4\right)$$

$$= 84\pi\,\text{cm}^3$$

Spheres

- A sphere is a 3D shape that is round, like a ball. At every point, its surface is equidistant from its centre.

Volume of a Sphere = $\frac{4}{3}\pi r^3$

Surface Area of a Sphere = $4\pi r^2$

- A hemisphere is half of a sphere; a dome with a circular base.

Work out a) the volume and b) the surface area of the sphere. Leave your answers in terms of π.

a) $V = \frac{4}{3} \times \pi \times 6^3 = 288\pi\,\text{cm}^3$

b) $SA = 4 \times \pi \times 6^2 = 144\pi\,\text{cm}^2$

Composite Shapes

Calculate the area of the shaded region.

$$A = (6 \times 7) - (\pi \times 1.5^2)$$

$$= 34.9\,\text{cm}^2 \text{ (to 1 d.p.)}$$

Find the area of the rectangle and subtract the area of the circle.

Key Point

To find the volume of a composite shape, you must break the shape down.

Work out the volume of the shape. Give your answer in terms of π.

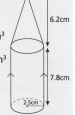

Volume of the cylinder = $2.5^2 \times \pi \times 7.8 = \frac{195}{4}\pi\,\text{cm}^3$

Volume of the cone = $\frac{1}{3} \times \pi \times 2.5^2 \times 6.2 = \frac{155}{12}\pi\,\text{cm}^3$

Total volume = $\frac{195}{4}\pi + \frac{155}{12}\pi = \frac{185}{3}\pi\,\text{cm}^3$

Quick Test

1. Work out the volume of a sphere with diameter 10cm.
2. Calculate the surface area of a cone with radius 3cm and perpendicular height 6cm.
3. Work out the volume of a square-based pyramid with side length 5cm and perpendicular height 8cm.
4. Calculate the surface area of a hemisphere with radius 6cm.

Key Words

pyramid
vertex / vertices
cone
frustum
sphere
hemisphere

Review Questions

Angles and Shapes 1 & 2

1 The three interior angles of a triangle are $y°$, $2y°$ and $3y°$.

Work out the size of the largest angle. 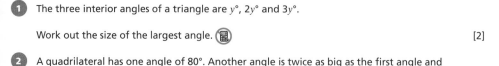 [2]

2 A quadrilateral has one angle of 80°. Another angle is twice as big as the first angle and a third angle is 20° smaller than the first angle.

Work out the size of the fourth angle. [2]

3 This angle diagram is incorrect. Explain why. [1]

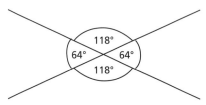

118°
64°   64°
118°

4 An aircraft flies from airport A on a bearing of 054° to airport B.

Work out the bearing that the aircraft must follow in order to return to airport A. [1]

5 Work out the exterior angle of a regular 15-sided shape. [2]

6 An irregular hexagon has interior angles in degrees of $2h$, $4h$, $4h$, $4h$, $5h$ and $5h$.

Work out the size of the smallest angle. [3]

7 State whether each of the following statements is **true** or **false**.

a) The sum of the interior angles of a heptagon is 900°. [1]

b) A parallelogram has no lines of symmetry and rotational symmetry of order 2. [1]

c) The direction south-east is on a bearing of 145°. [1]

> **Total Marks** .... / 14

Transformations & Constructions

1 **a)** Plot the following points: $A(2, 0)$ $B(5, 0)$ $C(5, 2)$ $D(3, 2)$ $E(3, 5)$ $F(2, 5)$
Join the points together and label the shape M.   [1]

     b) Rotate shape M by 180° about the origin to form shape N.   [1]

     c) Reflect shape N in the x-axis to form shape O.   [1]

     d) Describe fully the single transformation that maps shape O to shape M.   [2]

2 Rectangle R has a width of 3cm and a length of 5cm. It is enlarged by scale factor 3 to give rectangle T.

     a) What is the area of rectangle T?   [2]

     b) How many times bigger is the area of rectangle T than the area of rectangle R?   [2]

3 Describe how to construct an angle of 45°.   [2]

4 Describe the locus of points in the following:

     a) A person sitting on the London Eye as it rotates around.   [1]

     b) The seat of a moving swing.   [1]

     c) The end of the minute hand on a clock moving for one hour.   [1]

     d) The end of a moving see-saw.   [1]

5 The diagram represents a solid made from 10 identical cubes.
On a squared grid, draw the:

     a) Front elevation   [1]

     b) Plan view.   [1]

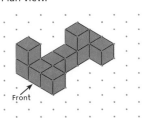

Front

Total Marks _____ / 17

Practice Questions

Transformations & Constructions

1

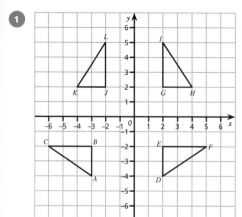

Describe the single transformation that maps:

a) Triangle *ABC* onto triangle *DEF*.

_____

_____ [2]

b) Triangle *DEF* onto triangle *GHI*.

_____

_____ [3]

c) Triangle *DEF* onto triangle *JKL*.

_____

_____ [2]

2 Using a pair of compasses and a ruler, mark two points, *C* and *D*, that are 5cm apart.

Draw the locus of points that are equidistant from *C* and *D*.

[2]

3 Draw any triangle *ABC*.

Construct the bisectors of each angle using a pair of compasses and a ruler.

[3]

Total Marks _____ / 12

Area and Volume 1 & 2

1. Two identical circles sit inside a square of side length 6cm.

    Work out the area of the shaded region. [4]

2. A vase is made from two cylinders. The larger cylinder has a radius of 15cm.
    The total volume of the vase is 6000πcm³.
    The ratio of volumes of the smaller cylinder to the larger cylinder is 1 : 3

    a) Calculate the height of the larger cylinder. [3]

    b) The height and radius of the smaller cylinder are equal. Work out the radius of the
       smaller cylinder. [3]

3. A cat's toy is made out of plastic.
    The top of the toy is a solid cone with radius 3cm and height 7cm.
    The bottom of the toy is a solid hemisphere. The base of the hemisphere and the base of the
    cone are the same size.

    Calculate the volume of plastic needed to make the toy. Give your answer in terms of π. [3]

4. The diagram below is the cross-section of a swimming pool.

    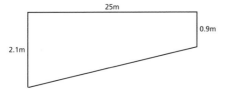

    The swimming pool is 10m wide. The pool fills at a rate of 0.2m³ per second.

    How many hours does it take to fill the pool completely?
    Give your answer to 3 significant figures.

    Answer _____ [4]

Total Marks _____ / 17

Congruence and Geometrical Problems

You must be able to:

- Identify congruent and similar shapes
- State the criteria that congruent triangles satisfy
- Solve problems involving similar figures
- Understand geometrical problems.

Congruent Triangles

- If two shapes are the same size and shape, they are congruent.
- Two triangles are congruent if they satisfy one of the following four criteria:
  - SSS – three sides are the same
  - SAS – two sides and the included angle (the angle between the two sides) are the same
  - ASA – two angles and one corresponding side are the same
  - RHS – there is a right angle, and the hypotenuse and one other corresponding side are the same.
- Sometimes angles or lengths of sides have to be calculated before congruency can be proved.

State whether these two triangles are congruent and give a reason for your answer.

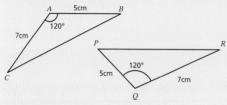

Angle CAB = Angle PQR (given)
$AC = QR$ (given)
$AB = PQ$ (given)
Triangles ABC and PQR are congruent because they satisfy the criteria SAS.

Key Point

Congruent shapes can be reflected, rotated or translated and remain congruent.

Similar Triangles

- Similar figures are identical in shape but can differ in size.
- In similar triangles:
  - corresponding angles are identical
  - lengths of corresponding sides are in the same ratio $y : z$
  - the area ratio $= y^2 : z^2$
  - the volume ratio $= y^3 : z^3$.

Triangles AED and ABC are similar.

Calculate **a)** AC and **b)** DC.

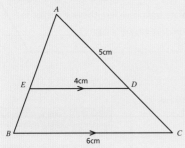

a) $\dfrac{4}{6} = \dfrac{5}{AC}$ ← The corresponding sides of both triangles are in the same ratio.

$4 \times AC = 6 \times 5$ ← Cross multiply.

$AC = \dfrac{6 \times 5}{4}$

$= 7.5\text{cm}$

b) $DC = AC - AD$

$= 7.5 - 5$

$= 2.5\text{cm}$

Geometrical Problems

- Congruency and similarity are used in many geometric proofs.

Prove that the base angles of an isosceles triangle are equal.

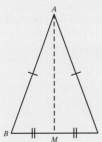

Given $\triangle ABC$ with $AB = AC$

Let M be the midpoint of BC

Join AM

$AB = AC$ (given)

$BM = MC$ (from construction)

$AM = AM$ (common side)

$\triangle ABM$ and $\triangle ACM$ are congruent (SSS)

So, angle ABC = angle ACB

> **Key Point**
>
> When writing a proof, always give a reason for each statement.

1.

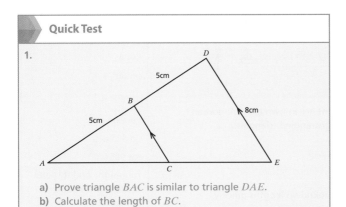

a) Prove triangle BAC is similar to triangle DAE.

b) Calculate the length of BC.

> **Key Words**
>
> congruent
> included angle
> similar

Right-Angled Triangles

You must be able to:

- Recall and use the formula for Pythagoras' Theorem
- Recall the trigonometric ratios
- Use the trigonometric ratios to calculate unknown lengths and angles in right-angled triangles in two and three-dimensional figures.

Pythagoras' Theorem

- Pythagoras' Theorem states $a^2 + b^2 = c^2$.
- The longest side (c) is opposite the right angle and called the **hypotenuse**.

LEARN

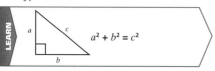

$$a^2 + b^2 = c^2$$

> Careful: b is a shorter side so the answer must be **less** than 14.1cm.

> Unless stated otherwise, give the answer to 3 significant figures.

Work out the length of the hypotenuse (c).

$3^2 + 4^2 = c^2$
$9 + 16 = c^2$
$c = \sqrt{25}$
$c = 5$m

Work out the length of b.

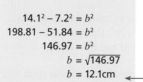

$14.1^2 - 7.2^2 = b^2$
$198.81 - 51.84 = b^2$
$146.97 = b^2$
$b = \sqrt{146.97}$
$b = 12.1$cm

A boat sails 15km due north, then 10km due east.

How far is the boat from its starting point? Give your answer to 3 decimal places.

$15^2 + 10^2 = c^2$
$225 + 100 = c^2$
$c = 18.028$km

- The following length combinations are known as Pythagorean triples and regularly appear in right-angled triangles:
  - (3, 4, 5)
  - (6, 8, 10)
  - (5, 12, 13)
  - (7, 24, 25).
- Memorise them to help identify unknown lengths quickly.

> ### Key Point
>
> You need to know the exact values of the trigonometric ratios for common angles:
>
> $\sin 0° = 0$
>
> $\cos 0° = 1$
>
> $\tan 0° = 0$
>
> $\sin 30° = \frac{1}{2}$
>
> $\cos 30° = \frac{\sqrt{3}}{2}$
>
> $\tan 30° = \frac{1}{\sqrt{3}}$
>
> $\sin 45° = \frac{1}{\sqrt{2}}$
>
> $\cos 45° = \frac{1}{\sqrt{2}}$
>
> $\tan 45° = 1$
>
> $\sin 60° = \frac{\sqrt{3}}{2}$
>
> $\cos 60° = \frac{1}{2}$
>
> $\tan 60° = \sqrt{3}$
>
> $\sin 90° = 1$
>
> $\cos 90° = 0$
>
> You might find it useful to learn the decimal values too.

$ABCDEFGH$ is a cuboid.
Calculate the length of AH to 2 decimal places.

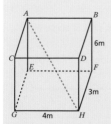
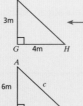
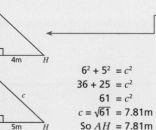

This is a Pythagorean triple, so $EH = 5$m.

$$6^2 + 5^2 = c^2$$
$$36 + 25 = c^2$$
$$61 = c^2$$
$$c = \sqrt{61} = 7.81\text{m}$$
$$\text{So } AH = 7.81\text{m}$$

Key Point

a^2 means $a \times a$ **not** $2 \times a$.

Key Point

Sine, cosine and tangent ratios can **only** be used in right-angled triangles.

Trigonometric Ratios

- You can calculate unknown sides or angles in right-angled triangles using sine, cosine and tangent.
- θ is a Greek letter called theta. It stands for the unknown angle.

$$\sin \theta = \frac{\text{Opposite}}{\text{Hypotenuse}} \quad \cos \theta = \frac{\text{Adjacent}}{\text{Hypotenuse}} \quad \tan \theta = \frac{\text{Opposite}}{\text{Adjacent}}$$

- The above formulae can be remembered by:

  Some **O**ld **H**orses **C**arry **A** **H**eavy **T**on **O**f **A**pples

  SOH   **CAH**   **TOA**

- For example, $\sin \theta$ (**S**ome) = $\dfrac{\text{Opposite (Old)}}{\text{Hypotenuse (Horses)}}$

OPP
(opposite the angle)

HYP
(longest side)

ADJ
(between the right angle and θ)

Work out x to 1 decimal place.

In this example you are looking for a missing length.

$$\sin 40° = \frac{x}{7}$$
$$x = 7 \times \sin 40°$$
$$x = 7 \times 0.6428 = 4.499...$$
$$x = 4.5\text{cm}$$

Work out θ to the nearest degree.

In this example you are looking for a missing angle.

On the calculator press either

$$\tan \theta = \frac{8}{5} = 1.6$$
$$\tan^{-1} 1.6 = 57.99°$$
$$\theta = 58°$$

Key Words

Pythagoras' Theorem
hypotenuse
sine
cosine
tangent
theta
opposite
adjacent

Quick Test

1. An isosceles triangle has side lengths of 7cm, 7cm and 5cm. Calculate the angle between the two equal sides to the nearest degree.
2. A triangle has sides 8cm, 15cm and 17cm. Is it right-angled?
3. ABC is a right-angled triangle, where angle $B = 90°$. $AB = 6$cm, $AC = 9$cm. Calculate BC to 2 decimal places.

Sine and Cosine Rules

You must be able to:

- Recall and use the sine rule to work out an unknown side or angle of a triangle
- Recall and use the cosine rule to work out an unknown side or angle of a triangle
- Recall and use Area $= \frac{1}{2}ab$ sin C to calculate the area, sides or angles of a triangle.

Solving Any Triangle

- The **sine rule** is used to calculate unknown angles or side lengths in triangles that are not right-angled.

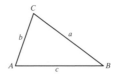

> **Key Point**
>
> Capital letters are used to represent angles; lower case letters are used to represent sides.

 Sine Rule: $\dfrac{a}{\sin A} = \dfrac{b}{\sin B} = \dfrac{c}{\sin C}$

Calculate the size of angle C.

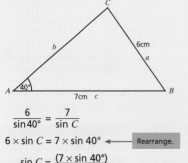

$$\frac{6}{\sin 40°} = \frac{7}{\sin C}$$

$6 \times \sin C = 7 \times \sin 40°$ ◄— Rearrange.

$\sin C = \dfrac{(7 \times \sin 40°)}{6}$

$\sin C = \dfrac{4.499513268}{6}$

$\sin C = 0.749918878$

$C = \sin^{-1} 0.749918878$ ◄— Always check your calculator is in degree mode.

$C = 48.58°$

Calculate the length of side BC to 2 decimal places.

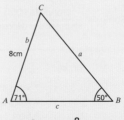

$$\frac{a}{\sin 71°} = \frac{8}{\sin 50°}$$ ◄— BC is side a.

$a \times \sin 50° = 8 \times \sin 71°$

$a = \dfrac{(8 \times \sin 71°)}{\sin 50°}$

$a = \dfrac{(8 \times 0.9455185756)}{0.7660444431}$

$a = \dfrac{7.564148605}{0.7660444431}$

$a = 9.87$cm (to 2 d.p.)

- The **cosine rule** is used for triangles without a right angle when:
  - two sides and the included angle (between them) are known
  - three sides are known.

 Cosine Rule: $a^2 = b^2 + c^2 - 2bc \cos A$ **OR** $\cos A = \dfrac{\left(b^2 + c^2 - a^2\right)}{2bc}$

Calculate the size of angle A to 1 decimal place.

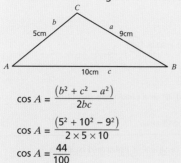

$$\cos A = \frac{(b^2 + c^2 - a^2)}{2bc}$$

$$\cos A = \frac{(5^2 + 10^2 - 9^2)}{2 \times 5 \times 10}$$

$$\cos A = \frac{44}{100}$$

$$\cos A = 0.44$$

Angle $A = \cos^{-1} 0.44$

Angle $A = 63.9°$

Calculate the length of side BC to 2 decimal places.

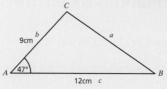

$a^2 = b^2 + c^2 - 2bc \cos A$ ← BC is side a.

$a^2 = 9^2 + 12^2 - 2 \times 9 \times 12 \times \cos 47°$

$a^2 = 225 - 216 \times \cos 47°$

$a^2 = 225 - 147.31$

$a^2 = 77.69$

$a = \sqrt{77.69}$

$a = 8.81$cm (to 2 d.p.)

Using Sine to Calculate the Area of a Triangle

- This formula for calculating the area of any triangle can be rearranged to work out unknown sides and angles:

Area $= \frac{1}{2}ab \sin C = \frac{1}{2}bc \sin A = \frac{1}{2}ac \sin B$

Key Point

If Area $= \frac{1}{2}ab \sin C$, then

$$a = \frac{2 \times \text{Area}}{b \sin C} \text{ and}$$

$$b = \frac{2 \times \text{Area}}{a \sin C}$$

$$\sin C = \frac{2 \times \text{Area}}{ab}$$

The area of the triangle ABC is 35.27cm².
Calculate the length of AC.
Give your answer to the nearest whole number.

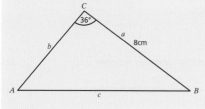

Area $= \frac{1}{2}ab \sin C$ ← Rearrange to make b (AC) the subject.

$$\frac{2 \times \text{Area}}{a \sin C} = b$$

$$\frac{2 \times 35.27}{8 \times \sin 36°} = b$$

$$\frac{70.54}{4.7023} = b$$

$$b = AC = 15\text{cm}$$

Quick Test

1. In triangle ABC, angle $A = 44°$, angle $C = 64°$ and $BC = 4$cm.
   Calculate a) the length of AB and b) the area of triangle ABC to 3 decimal places.

Key Words

sine rule
cosine rule

Review Questions

Transformations & Constructions

1 Three points $X(5,1)$, $Y(3, 5)$ and $Z(1, 2)$ are reflected in the y-axis.

    a) Give the new coordinates of the three points. [3]

    b) The original points X, Y and Z are rotated 90° about (0, 0) in a clockwise direction.

        Give the coordinates of the three points in their new positions. [3]

2 A rectangle (C) measures 3cm by 5.5cm. Each length of rectangle C is enlarged by scale factor 3 to form a new rectangle (D).

    What is the ratio of the area of rectangle C to rectangle D? [3]

3 Describe the locus of points for the following:

    a) The path of a rocket for the first three seconds after take-off. [1]

    b) A point just below the handle on an opening door. [1]

    c) The central point of a bicycle wheel as the bicycle travels along a level road. [1]

    d) The end of a pendulum on a grandfather clock. [1]

4 Describe the plan view of a cube measuring 4cm by 4cm by 4cm. [1]

5 A can of baked beans has a circular lid of circumference 22cm and a height of 8cm.

    Draw the side elevation of the tin when it is standing upright. (Take π as $\frac{22}{7}$) [2]

6 The photograph shows a World War II Lancaster Bomber.

    Sketch:

    a) The side elevation of the Lancaster Bomber [2]

    b) The front elevation of the Lancaster Bomber [2]

    c) The plan view of the Lancaster Bomber. [2]

Total Marks .... / 22

Transformations & Constructions

1 On the grid below plot the points: $A(2, 1)$, $B(4, 1)$ and $C(3, 5)$. Join the points together. Using construction lines, enlarge triangle ABC by scale factor 2, centre of enlargement $(0, 0)$, to form triangle DEF.

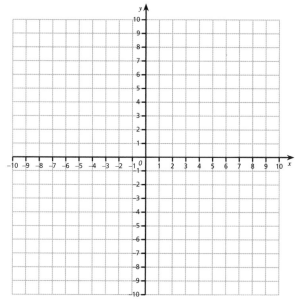

[3]

2 A pyramid has a rectangular base 3cm by 4cm and a height of 5cm.

Draw an accurate plan view of the pyramid. 📱

[2]

Total Marks _____ / 5

Area and Volume 1 & 2

1 a) Work out the volume of the triangular prism. [2]

   b) A cube has the same volume as the triangular prism.

      Work out the total length of all the edges of the cube. [3]

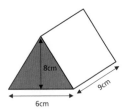

2 The numerical values of the area and circumference of a circle are equal.

   Work out the radius of this circle. [2]

3 The volume of the trapezoid is 900cm³.
   All measurements are in centimetres.

   Work out the value of x. [4]

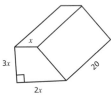

4 The ratio of the radius to the height of a cylinder is 1 : 3
   The volume of the cylinder is 275πcm³.

   Calculate the value of the radius. Give your answer to 3 significant figures.

Answer _____ [4]

Total Marks _____ / 15

Congruence and Geometrical Problems

1 Prove that triangle ABC and triangle BCD are similar. [3]

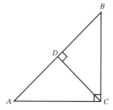

2 The corresponding lengths of two cuboids are 12cm and 3cm.

What is the ratio of their volumes? Circle your answer.

64 : 1   4 : 1   8 : 1   1 : 4   [1]

3 Here are four triangles, A, B, C and D.

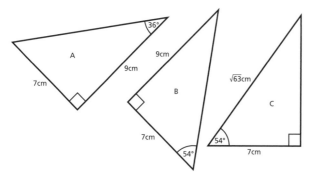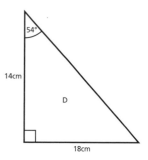

a) Which two triangles are congruent? Give a reason for your answer.

Answer _____ [2]

b) Which triangles are similar to triangle A?

Answer _____ [1]

Total Marks _____ / 7

Practice Questions

Right-Angled Triangles

1 A man walks 6.7km due north. He then turns due west and walks 7.6km.

How far is he now from his starting point? [3]

2 A 4m ladder leans against a vertical wire fence. The foot of the ladder is 2m from the base of the fence. Fang, the lion, can jump 3m vertically.

Will Fang be able to jump over the fence?
You must give reasons for your answer. [4]

3 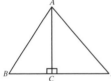 AB = 10cm, BC = 8cm and CD = 6cm.

a) Calculate AD to 3 significant figures. [3]

b) What type of triangle is triangle ABD? [1]

4 A bumblebee leaves its nest and flies 10 metres due south and then 6 metres due west.

What is the shortest distance the bumblebee has to fly to return to its nest?
Give your answer to 3 significant figures. [3]

5 A triangle has side lengths of 1.5cm, 2.5cm and 2cm. Is it a right-angled triangle?
Explain your answer. [3]

6 How long is the diagonal of a square of side length 3cm? [2]

7 A regular hexagon is inscribed in a circle of radius 6cm.

Use sine to prove that the side length of the hexagon is 6cm. [2]

8 A is the point (4, 0) and B is the point (7, 5).

Calculate the angle between AB and the x-axis to the nearest degree. [2]

9 A lifeguard is at the top of a lookout tower of height 14m, situated on a small island.
She sees a swimmer (P) due west of her at an angle of depression of 35°.
She sees another swimmer (Q) due south at an angle of depression of 18°.
Work out:

a) The distance of swimmer P from the base of the tower. [2]

b) The distance of swimmer Q from the base of the tower. [2]

c) The shortest distance between swimmers P and Q. Give your answer to 1 decimal place. [2]

Total Marks _____ / 29

Sine and Cosine Rules

1 In a triangle ABC, AC = 5.7cm and AB = 7.5cm. The area of the triangle is 20cm².

Calculate angle CAB to the nearest degree. [4]

2 ABC is a triangle where BC = 12cm and CA = 14cm.

If angle ABC = 50°, calculate angle BAC to 2 decimal places. [3]

3 A tourist was standing 30m from the base of the Leaning Tower of Pisa.
The angle of elevation to the top of the tower was 30°.
The distance of the tourist from the top of the tower was 80m.

Calculate the slanting height (l) of the Leaning Tower of Pisa.
Give your answer to the nearest metre. [5]

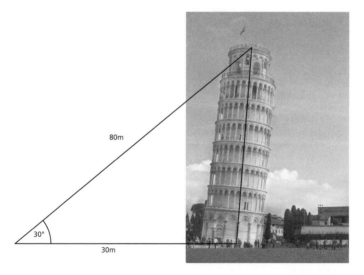

4 In a golf championship, the distance from the tee to the third hole is 250m.
A golfer hits the ball 220m and it ends up 78m from the hole.

Calculate the angle (from the tee) that the ball went off course to 2 decimal places. [2]

Total Marks _____ / 14

Circles

You must be able to:

- Identify and use different properties of circles
- Apply and prove theorems relating to circles
- Understand cyclic quadrilaterals.

Circle Theorems

- The angle subtended (formed) at the centre of a circle is twice the angle at the circumference if both are subtended from the same chord or arc.

- Angles subtended from the same chord or arc to the circumference are equal.

- Any angle subtended from each end of the diameter will be 90°.

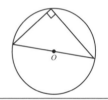

Cyclic Quadrilaterals

- All four corners of a cyclic quadrilateral touch the circumference of the circle.
- Opposite angles of a cyclic quadrilateral add up to 180°.

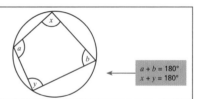

$a + b = 180°$
$x + y = 180°$

Tangents and Chords

- A tangent is a straight line that touches the circumference of the circle at a single point.
- If a tangent and a radius meet at a point on the circumference, the angle between them is 90°.

- If two tangents are drawn from the same external point to a circle, they will be of equal lengths.
  $AB = AC$
  Triangle OAB and triangle OAC are congruent.

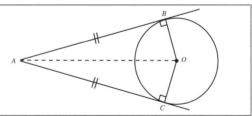

- The line joining the centre of the circle to the midpoint of a chord is perpendicular to the chord.

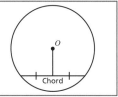

Sectors

- The sector of a circle is a section of the circle bounded by two radii and an arc.
- If the angle at the centre is θ then:

Sector Area $= \dfrac{\theta}{360} \times \pi r^2$

Arc Length of Sector $= \dfrac{\theta}{360} \times 2\pi r$

Alternate Segment Theorem

- The angle between the tangent and the chord is equal to the angle subtended by the chord in the alternate segment.

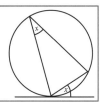

> **Quick Test**

1. Work out the size of the lettered angle in each diagram.

a)

b)

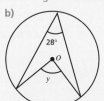

c)

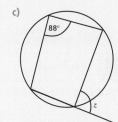

d)

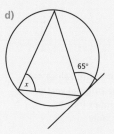

Vectors

You must be able to:

- Add and subtract vectors
- Multiply a vector by a scalar
- Work out the magnitude of a vector
- Use vectors in geometric arguments and proofs.

Properties of Vectors

- A **vector** is a quantity that has both **magnitude** (size) and direction.
- Vectors are equal only when they have equal magnitudes and are in the same direction.

> **Key Point**
>
> The direction of a vector is shown by an arrow.

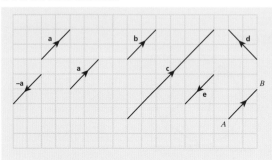

$\mathbf{b} = \mathbf{a}$ (same direction, same length)

$\mathbf{d} \neq \mathbf{a}$ (different direction, same length)

$\mathbf{e} = -\mathbf{a}$ (opposite direction, same length)

$\mathbf{c} = 3\mathbf{a}$ (same direction, 3 × length of a)

$\mathbf{a} = \overrightarrow{AB} = \underline{a} = \begin{pmatrix} 2 \\ 2 \end{pmatrix}$ ← These are all ways of writing the same vector.

$-\mathbf{a} = \begin{pmatrix} -2 \\ -2 \end{pmatrix}$

a and **c** are parallel vectors.
a and **b** are equal vectors.

- Any number of vectors can be added together.

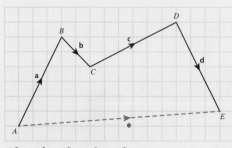

$\mathbf{a} + \mathbf{b} + \mathbf{c} + \mathbf{d} = \begin{pmatrix} 3 \\ 6 \end{pmatrix} + \begin{pmatrix} 2 \\ -2 \end{pmatrix} + \begin{pmatrix} 6 \\ 3 \end{pmatrix} + \begin{pmatrix} 3 \\ -6 \end{pmatrix}$

$= \begin{pmatrix} 14 \\ 1 \end{pmatrix}$

$\overrightarrow{AB} + \overrightarrow{BC} + \overrightarrow{CD} + \overrightarrow{DE} = \overrightarrow{AE}$ or **e** ← ——————————— This is the resultant vector.

- When a vector is multiplied by a **scalar** (a numerical value), the resultant vector will always be parallel to the original vector.
- When a vector is multiplied by a positive number (not 1), the direction of the vector does not change, only its magnitude.

> **Key Point**
>
> The sum of the lengths $AB + BC + CD + DE$ does **not** equal the length of AE.

- When a vector is multiplied by a negative number (not –1), the magnitude of the vector changes and the vector points in the opposite direction.
- The magnitude of a vector **a** is written $|a|$
- Magnitude of vector $\begin{pmatrix} x \\ y \end{pmatrix}$ is $\sqrt{x^2 + y^2}$

Work out the magnitude of vector **a**.

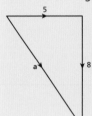

Vector $\mathbf{a} = \begin{pmatrix} 5 \\ -8 \end{pmatrix}$

$a^2 = 5^2 + 8^2$ ◄———————— Use Pythagoras' Theorem.

$a^2 = 25 + 64$

$|a| = \sqrt{89}$

$|a| = 9.43$ (to 3 significant figures)

Vectors in Geometry

- All rules of algebra can be applied to vector expressions.

In triangle *DEF*, *G* and *H* are the midpoints of *DE* and *DF*.

Prove that $GH = \frac{1}{2}EF$ and that *GH* is parallel to *EF*.

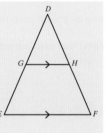

Let $\overrightarrow{DE} = \mathbf{e}$ and $\overrightarrow{DF} = \mathbf{f}$

So, $\overrightarrow{EF} = \overrightarrow{ED} + \overrightarrow{DF}$

$\qquad = -\mathbf{e} + \mathbf{f} = \mathbf{f} - \mathbf{e}$

Also $\overrightarrow{DG} = \frac{1}{2}\overrightarrow{DE} = \frac{1}{2}\mathbf{e}$

$\qquad \overrightarrow{DH} = \frac{1}{2}\overrightarrow{DF} = \frac{1}{2}\mathbf{f}$

So, $\overrightarrow{GH} = \overrightarrow{GD} + \overrightarrow{DH}$

$\qquad = -\frac{1}{2}\mathbf{e} + \frac{1}{2}\mathbf{f} = \frac{1}{2}\mathbf{f} - \frac{1}{2}\mathbf{e} = \frac{1}{2}(\mathbf{f} - \mathbf{e})$

$\overrightarrow{GH} = \frac{1}{2}\overrightarrow{EF}$

Therefore, $GH = \frac{1}{2}EF$ and *GH* is parallel to *EF*. ◄———— This is called the midpoint theorem.

▶ **Quick Test**

1. Vector **a** has a magnitude of 3cm and a direction of 120°.
   Vector **b** has a magnitude of 4cm and a direction of 040°.
   Draw the vectors:
   a) **a**   b) **b**   c) –**a**   d) 2**a**   e) **a** + **b**

▶ **Key Words**

vector
magnitude
scalar

Review Questions

Congruence and Geometrical Problems

1 A triangle has angles of 56°, 64° and 60°. The triangle is enlarged by scale factor 2.

What are the angles of the enlarged triangle? [3]

2 In triangle ABC, AB = 10cm, BC = 12cm and CA = 10cm.

a) What type of triangle is triangle ABC? [1]

b) D is a point on BC such that AD is the perpendicular bisector of BC.

Prove that triangle ABD is congruent to triangle ACD. [3]

c) Calculate the area of triangle ABC.

Answer _____ [3]

3 A man who is 1.6m tall is standing by a lamp post. He casts a shadow that is 2.8m long.

Work out the height of a lamp post that casts a shadow 38m long.
Give your answer to 1 decimal place.

Answer _____ [2]

4 Two mugs, A and B, are similar. Mug A has a height of 10cm and mug B has a height of 8cm. Mug A has a volume of 36cm³.

Work out the volume of mug B to the nearest cm³.

Answer _____ [3]

Total Marks _____ / 15

Right-Angled Triangles

1 One of the pyramids of Egypt is built on a square base of width 200m.

C is the centre of the base. The slant height *TB* is 310m.

Work out the perpendicular height of the pyramid to the nearest metre. [4]

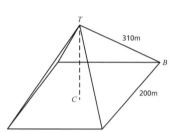

2 A rectangle measures 3cm by 4cm.

What is the length of its diagonal? Circle your answer.

5cm $\sqrt{14}$cm   12cm   14cm [1]

3 Calculate the area of the triangle. [3]

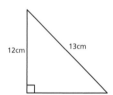

4 *PCDEF* is a pyramid with a rectangular base *CDEF*.
CD = 8cm and DE = 5cm.
P is vertically above the centre of the rectangle and PC = PD = PE = PF = 13cm.

Calculate:

a) The angle between *PC* and the plane *CDEF*. Give your answer to 1 decimal place. [4]

b) The vertical height of *P* above the rectangular base. Give your answer to 3 significant figures. [2]

5 Two polar bears, Snowy and Blizzard, are asleep in an enclosure.
The distance from Snowy to Blizzard is 25m. The bearing of Blizzard from Snowy is 078°.

Calculate how far east Blizzard is from Snowy. Give your answer to 2 decimal places. [2]

Total Marks _____ / 16

Sine and Cosine Rules

1 Here is a triangle ABC.

a) Which angle is the smallest?
Give a reason for your answer. [2]

b) Calculate the size of the smallest angle to the nearest degree. [4]

c) Calculate the area of triangle ABC. [3]

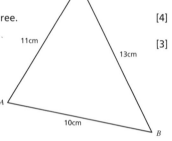

2 A fishing boat leaves harbour and sails 12km on a bearing of 040° to a lighthouse.

The boat then changes direction and sails on a bearing of 145° to visit Seal Island, which is 14km due east from the harbour.

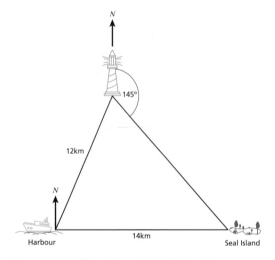

How far is Seal Island from the lighthouse?
Give your answer to 1 decimal place. [4]

Total Marks _____ / 13

Circles

1. For each of the following questions, work out the lettered angles.
The centre of each circle (where appropriate) is marked with an *O*. 📠

a) [1]

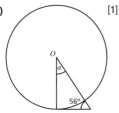

b) [2]

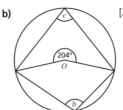

c) [2]

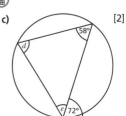

d) [2]

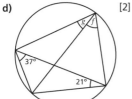

e) [2]

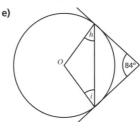

f) [1]

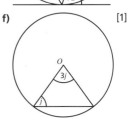

> **Total Marks** _____ / 10

Vectors

1. *ABC* is a triangle. *D* is the midpoint of *AB*. *E* is the midpoint of *BC*.
$\overrightarrow{AB}$ = **a** and $\overrightarrow{AC}$ = **c**

a) Work out $\overrightarrow{AE}$ in terms of **a** and **c**. [3]

b) Show that $\overrightarrow{DE}$ is parallel to $\overrightarrow{AC}$. [3]

2. State whether the following can best be described as a vector or as a scalar:

a) The length of a desk [1]

b) The flight path of an aircraft [1]

c) A snooker ball hit directly into a pocket. [1]

> **Total Marks** _____ / 9

Review Questions

Circles

1 Work out the size of the angle marked with a letter. The centre of each circle (where appropriate) is marked with an O. 🖩

a) [1]

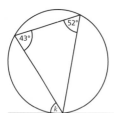

b) [1]

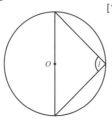

c) [2]

2 a) Label each arrow pointing to a different part of the circle. [5]

b) Calculate the length of c if the radius = 10cm (Take $\pi = 3.14$)
Give your answer to 2 decimal places. [3]

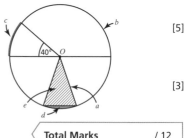

⟨ **Total Marks** _____ / 12 ⟩

Vectors

1 Which of these vectors will be parallel to **4a + 3b**? Circle your answer.

4a + 6b   8a + 3b   8a + 6b   4a – 3b   [1]

2 $ABCD$ is a parallelogram and $\overrightarrow{AC}$ is one of the diagonals.
P is a point on $\overrightarrow{AC}$ such that $\overrightarrow{AP} = \frac{1}{4}\overrightarrow{AC}$
$\overrightarrow{DA} = $ **4a** and $\overrightarrow{DC} = $ **4c**

a) Work out the vector $\overrightarrow{AC}$ in terms of **a** and **c**. [1]

b) Work out the vector $\overrightarrow{AP}$ in terms of **a** and **c**. [1]

c) Work out the vector $\overrightarrow{DP}$ in terms of **a** and **c**. [1]

3 Write down whether each of these statements is **true** or **false**.

a) Velocity is a vector. [1]

b) Two vectors are equal if they have the same magnitude but are in opposite directions. [1]

⟨ **Total Marks** _____ / 6 ⟩

Answers

Page 5 Quick Test
1. a) Rectangle, Parallelogram, Kite
    b) Square, Rhombus
2. Angle $EJH = 16°$

Page 7 Quick Test
1. a) 3240°
    b) 162°
2. 12
3.

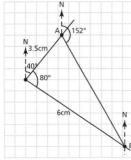

Bearing = 152° ± 2°

Page 8
1.

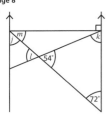

(Marks will not be awarded if reason is incorrect.) $j = 72°$ (alternate angle) **[1]**;
$k = 54°$ (sum of the interior angles of a triangle = 180°) **[1]**; $l = 54°$
(vertically opposite angles are equal) **[1]**;
$m = 18°$ (90° − 72°) **[1]**
2. a) Angle DCB = Angle DAB = 110°
    (opposite angles in a parallelogram
    are equal) **[1]**
    b) Angle ABC = 70° (allied angle to
    Angle BAD) **[1]**
3. $9x = 360°$, $x = 40°$ **[1]**;
    largest angle = 120° **[1]**
4. Exterior angle = $\frac{360}{n} = \frac{360}{10} = 36°$ **[1]**;
    interior angle = 180° − 36° = 144° **[1]**
5. Bearing = 180° + 36° = 216° **[1]**
6. a) Number of sides = 360° ÷ exterior
    angle = 360 ÷ 45 = 8 **[1]**
    b) Octagon **[1]**

Page 9
1. $9x = 360°$ **[1]**; $x = 40°$ **[1]**
2. Exterior angle (= 180° − 150°) = 30° **[1]**;
    Number of sides = 360 ÷ 30 = 12 **[1]**

3. a) Correct scale drawing (see sketch
    below) **[1]**;
    Distance = 62km (+/− 2km) **[1]**

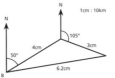

    b) Bearing 253° (± 2°) **[1]**

Page 11 Quick Test
1. a) A translation by the vector $\begin{pmatrix} 5 \\ -1 \end{pmatrix}$
    b) A reflection in the line $y = x$
    c) A rotation of 90° anticlockwise about
    (0, 0)

Page 13 Quick Test
1. Draw a line and mark on it two points,
    A and B.

    Open compasses to length AB.

    Put compass point on A and draw an
    arc. Put compass point on B and draw
    an arc.

    Draw a line to join A to the new
    point, C.

    Adjust compasses so less than
    length AB.

    Put compass point on A and draw
    arcs crossing AB and AC at points D
    and E.

    Put compass point on D and draw an
    arc. Put compass point on E and draw
    an arc. Draw a line from A to the new
    point, F.
2.

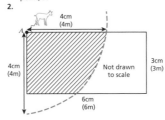

Page 15 Quick Test
1. Volume = 301.59cm³ (to 2 d.p.) and
    surface area = 251.33cm² (to 2 d.p.)
2. 24cm²
3. Circumference = 21.99cm (to 2 d.p.) and
    area = 38.48cm² (to 2 d.p.)

Page 17 Quick Test
1. $\frac{500\pi}{3}$ or 523.6cm³
2. 91.5cm²
3. $\frac{200}{3}$ or 66.7cm³
4. 108π or 339.3cm²

Page 18
1. $y + 2y + 3y = 180°$, $6y = 180°$, $y = 30°$ **[1]**;
    Largest angle = 90° **[1]**
2. 80° + 160° + 60° + fourth angle = 360° **[1]**;
    Angle = 60° **[1]**
3. Angles around a point add up to
    360°. These angles add up to 364°,
    so diagram is incorrect. **[1]**
4. Bearing = 180° + 054° = 234° **[1]**
5. Exterior angle = 360° ÷ n **[1]**;
    360° ÷ 15 = 24° **[1]**
6. Sum of interior angles (hexagon) =
    4 × 180° = 720° **[1]**; 24h = 720°,
    h = 30° **[1]**; Smallest angle (2h) =
    2 × 30° = 60° **[1]**
7. a) True **[1]**
    b) True **[1]**
    c) False **[1]**

Page 19
1.

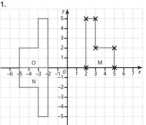

    a) Shape M plotted correctly **[1]**
    b) Shape N plotted correctly **[1]**
    c) Shape O plotted correctly **[1]**
    d) Reflection **[1]** in the y-axis OR
    mirror line $x = 0$ **[1]**
2. a) Rectangle T is 9cm × 15cm **[1]**;
    Area = 135cm² **[1]**
    b) Area R = 15cm², Area T = 135cm² **[1]**;
    T is 9 times bigger. **[1]**
3. Draw a line and construct the
    perpendicular bisector of the line. **[1]**;
    Bisect the right angle. **[1]**
4. a) A circle **[1]**
    b) An arc of a circle **[1]**
    c) A circle **[1]**
    d) An arc of a circle **[1]**
5. a) Front elevation

    [1]
    b) Plan view

    [1]

Answers

1. a) Reflection [1]; in line $x = -\frac{1}{2}$ [1]
   b) Rotation [1]; anticlockwise 90° [1]; centre of rotation (0, 0) [1]
   c) Reflection [1]; in line $y = x$ [1]
2. Correct construction of the perpendicular bisector of CD. [2]

3. Correct construction of the bisectors of the three angles. [3]

Page 21
1. Area of square $= 36\text{cm}^2$ [1]; Area of circles $= 2 \times \pi \times 1.5^2 = 14.137\ldots$ [1]; Shaded region $= 36 - 14.137\ldots$ [1]; $= 21.9\text{cm}^2$ (to 3 significant figures) [1]
2. a) Volume of large cylinder $= \frac{3}{4} \times 6000\pi = 4500\pi$ [1]; $4500\pi = \pi \times 15^2 \times h$ [1]; $h = 20\text{cm}$ [1]
   b) Volume of small cylinder $= \frac{1}{4} \times 6000\pi = 1500\pi$ [1]; $1500\pi = \pi \times r^2 \times h = \pi \times r^3$ [1]; $r = 11.4\text{cm}$ (to 3 significant figures) [1]
3. Volume of cone $= \frac{1}{3} \times \pi \times 3^2 \times 7 = 21\pi$ [1]; Volume of the hemisphere $= \frac{1}{2} \times \frac{4}{3} \times \pi \times 3^3 = 18\pi$ [1]; Volume of plastic needed $= 21\pi + 18\pi = 39\pi \text{ cm}^3$ [1]
4. Area of cross-section $= \frac{1}{2}(2.1+0.9) \times 25 = 37.5$, Volume $= 37.5 \times 10 = 375$ [1]; $375 \div 0.2 = 1875$ seconds [1]; $1875 \div 3600$ [1] $= 0.521$ hours (to 3 significant figures) [1]

3600 seconds = 1 hour

Pages 22–27 Revise Questions

Page 23 Quick Test
1. a) Angle ABC = Angle ADE (corresponding angles are equal); Angle ACB = Angle AED (corresponding angles are equal); Angle DAE is common to both triangles; so triangles are similar (three matching angles).
   b) $\frac{5}{10} = \frac{BC}{8}$ so $BC = 4\text{cm}$

Page 25 Quick Test
1. 42°
2. Yes, because $8^2 + 15^2 = 17^2$
3. 6.71cm

Page 27 Quick Test
1. a) $\frac{4}{\sin 44} = \frac{AB}{\sin 64}$; $AB = 5.175\text{cm}$
   b) Angle $B = 72°$, so area $= 9.844\text{cm}^2$

Pages 28–30 Review Questions

Page 28
1. a) $X = (-5, 1)$ [1]; $Y = (-3, 5)$ [1]; $Z = (-1, 2)$ [1]
   b) $X = (1, -5)$ [1]; $Y = (5, -3)$ [1]; $Z = (2, -1)$ [1]
2. Lengths of rectangle D: $(3 \times 3 =) 9\text{cm}$ and $(5.5 \times 3 =) 16.5\text{cm}$ [1]; Area of rectangle $C = 16.5\text{cm}^2$, Area of rectangle $D = 148.5\text{cm}^2$ [1]; Ratio is 1 : 9 [1]
3. a) A vertical line [1]
   b) An arc of a circle [1]
   c) A horizontal straight line [1]
   d) An arc of a circle [1]
4. A square 4cm × 4cm [1]
5. Diameter of lid = 7cm [1]; Diagram of a rectangle 7cm × 8cm [1]
6. a)  [2]
   b) [2]
   c) [2]

Page 29
1. One mark for each correct vertex of triangle DEF (all construction lines must be seen). [3]

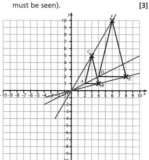

2. Accurate rectangle 3cm by 4cm [1]; Diagonals of rectangle drawn. [1]

Page 30
1. a) $\frac{1}{2} \times 6 \times 8 \times 9$ [1]; 216cm^3 [1]
   b) $\sqrt[3]{216} = 6$ [1]; 6×12 [1]; $= 72\text{cm}$
2. $\pi r^2 = 2\pi r$ [1]; $r = 2$ [1]
3. $\frac{1}{2}(2x + x) \times 3x \times 20 = 900$ [1]; $9x^2 = 90$ [1]; $x^2 = 10$ [1]; $x = \sqrt{10}$ or 3.16cm [1]
4. $h = 3r$ [1]; $\pi r^2(3r) = 275\pi$ [1]; $r = \sqrt[3]{\frac{275}{3}}$ [1]; $r = 4.51\text{cm}$ [1]

Pages 31–33 Practice Questions

Page 31
1. Angle ACB = Angle BDC = 90° [1]; Angle ABC = Angle DBC (the angle is common to both triangles) [1]; Angle BAC = Angle BCD (180° − Angle B − 90°), so the triangles are similar (three matching angles) [1]
2. 64 : 1 [1]
3. a) A and B [1]; AAS or SAS [1]
   b) B and D [1]

Page 32
1. $7.6^2 + 6.7^2 = y^2$ [1]; $57.76 + 44.89 = y^2$ [1]; $y = \sqrt{(102.65)} = 10.13\text{km}$ [1]
2. $4^2 - 2^2 = f^2$ [1]; $16 - 4 = f^2$ [1]; $\sqrt{12} = f$, fence height = 3.46m [1]; No, because the fence height is 3.46m and Fang can only jump 3m. [1]
3. a) AC is 6cm (Pythagorean triple) [1]; $6^2 + 6^2 = AD^2$ [1]; $\sqrt{72} = AD = 8.49\text{cm}$ (to 3 significant figures) [1]
   b) Scalene triangle [1]
4. $10^2 + 6^2 = b^2$ [1]; $100 + 36 = b^2$ [1]; $b = \sqrt{136} = 11.7\text{m}$ (to 3 significant figures) [1]
5. $1.5^2 + 2^2 = 6.25$ [1]; $\sqrt{6.25} = 2.5$ [1]; it is a right-angled triangle because Pythagoras' Theorem applies [1]
6. $3^2 + 3^2 = d^2$ [1]; $d = \sqrt{18} = 4.24\text{cm}$ [1]
7. $\sin 30° = \frac{x}{6}$ (where x is half the length of the hexagonal side) [1]; $x = 6 \times \sin 30° = 3\text{cm}$, so length of side = 6cm [1]
8. $\tan \theta = \frac{5}{3} = 1.6667$ [1]; $\theta = 59°$ [1]
9. a) Distance (x) of P from base of tower: $\tan 35° = \frac{14}{x}$, $x = \frac{14}{\tan 35°}$ [1]; $x = 19.9941\text{m}$ [1]
   b) Distance (y) of Q from base of tower: $\tan 18° = \frac{14}{y}$ [1]; $y = 43.0876\text{m}$ [1]
   c) $19.9941^2 + 43.0876^2 = PQ^2$, $399.764 + 1856.541 = PQ^2$ [1]; $PQ = 47.5\text{m}$ [1]

Answers

Page 33

1. Area $= \frac{1}{2}bc \sin A$,

   $20 = \frac{1}{2}(5.7 \times 7.5 \times \sin A)$ [1]; $\sin A =$
   $\frac{40}{42.75} = 0.9357$ [1]; Angle $CAB = 69.34°$
   [1]; Angle $CAB = 69°$ (to the nearest
   degree) [1]

2. $\frac{14}{\sin 50°} = \frac{12}{\sin A}$ [1];

   $\sin A = \left(\frac{12 \times \sin 50°}{14}\right)$ [1];

   Angle $BAC = 41.04°$ [1]

3. $a^2 = b^2 + c^2 - 2bc \cos A$ [1];
   $a^2 = 80^2 + 30^2 - 2 \times 80 \times 30 \times \cos 30°$ [1];
   $a^2 = 7300 - 4156.9$ [1]; $a = \sqrt{3143.1} =$
   56.06m [1]; Height of the Leaning
   Tower = 56m [1]

4. $\cos A = \frac{(b^2 + c^2 - a^2)}{2bc}$

   $= \frac{(220^2 + 250^2 - 78^2)}{2 \times 220 \times 250}$

   $= \frac{(104\,816)}{110\,000} = 0.95287...$ [1];

   $A = 17.66°$ [1]

Page 35 Quick Test

1. a) 32°   b) 56°
   c) 88°   d) 65°

Page 37 Quick Test

1. a)

   b)

   c)

   d)

   e)

Page 38

1. 56° [1]; 64° [1]; 60° [1]
2. a) Isosceles   [1]
   b) Prove using SSS OR SAS   [3]
   c) $AD^2 = 10^2 - 6^2$ [1]; $AD = 8$cm [1];
      Area $= \frac{1}{2}(12 \times 8) = 48$cm² [1]

3. $\frac{38}{2.8} = \frac{\text{lamp post height}}{1.6}$
   or $(38 \div 2.8) \times 1.6$ [1];
   = 21.7 metres [1]

4. Ratio of heights $= \frac{10}{8} = 1.25$ [1];
   Ratio of volumes = 1.25 × 1.25 × 1.25 [1];
   Volume of mug B = 36 ÷ 1.25³
   = 18.432 = 18cm³ [1];
   OR
   Ratio of heights = 1 : 0.8 [1];
   Ratio of volumes = 1 : 0.8³ [1];
   Volume of mug B = 36 × 0.8³
   = 18.432 =18cm³   [1]

Page 39

1. Diagonal length of base: 200² + 200² =
   d^2 [1]; $d = \sqrt{80000} = 282.84$m;
   $BC = 141.42$m [1];
   Using triangle TCB: 310² – 141.42² =
   TC^2 [1]; $TC = \sqrt{76\,100.38}$, $TC = 276$m [1]
2. 5cm   [1]
3. Third side of the triangle = 5cm
   (Pythagorean Triple) [1];
   Area $= \frac{1}{2}$ base × height, Area = 6 × 5 [1];
   Area = 30cm² [1]
4. a) 8² + 5² = CE^2 [1]; CE = 9.434cm [1];
      $\cos \theta = \frac{4.717}{13} = 0.36285$ [1]; θ = Angle
      PCE = 68.7° [1]
   b) 13² – 4.717² = h^2 [1]; Height of P
      above base = 12.1cm [1]
5. $\sin 78° = \frac{x}{25}$ [1]; x = 25 × sin 78°
   = 24.45m [1]

Page 40

1. a) Angle C is the smallest [1], because it
      is opposite the shortest side. [1]
   b) $\cos C = \frac{(a^2 + b^2 - c^2)}{2ab}$ [1];
      $\cos C = \frac{(13^2 + 11^2 - 10^2)}{2 \times 13 \times 11}$ [1]; cos C
      = 0.6643 [1]; Angle C = 48° (to the
      nearest degree) [1]
   c) Area $= \frac{1}{2}ab \sin C$ [1];
      Area $= \frac{1}{2} \times 13 \times 11 \times \sin 48°$ [1];
      Area = 53.13cm² [1]
2. $b^2 = a^2 + c^2 - 2ac \cos B$ [1];
   $b^2 = 144 + 196 - 2 \times 12 \times 14 \times \cos 50°$ [1];
   = 340 – 215.976 6369
   = 124.023 3631 [1];
   b = 11.1km [1] OR
   $\frac{14}{\sin 75°} = \frac{b}{\sin 50°}$ [1]; $b = \frac{(14 \times \sin 50°)}{\sin 75°}$ [1];
   $= \frac{10.724\,6222}{0.965\,925\,826}$ [1]; = 11.1 km[1]

Page 41

1. a) a = 34° (90° – 56°)   [1]
   b) b = 102° (204° ÷ 2) [1]; c = 78°
      (180° – 102°) [1]
   c) d = 72° (alternate segment) [1];
      e = 50° (180° – 72° – 58°) [1]
   d) f = 37° (angle subtended by a chord)
      [1]; g = 21° (angle subtended by a
      chord) [1]
   e) h = 42° (90° – ((180° – 84°) ÷ 2)
      = 90° – 48° = 42°) [1]; i = 42°
      (isosceles triangle) [1]
   f) j = 36° (isosceles triangle so 5j = 180°)
                                                 [1]

1. a) $a + \frac{1}{2}(c - a)$ [2];
      $\frac{1}{2}a + \frac{1}{2}c = \frac{1}{2}(a + c)$ [1]
   b) $\overrightarrow{DE} = \frac{1}{2}a + \frac{1}{2}(c - a)$ [1];
      $= \frac{1}{2}a + \frac{1}{2}c - \frac{1}{2}a = \frac{1}{2}c$ [1];
      $\overrightarrow{AC}$ = c, so $\overrightarrow{DE}$ is parallel to $\overrightarrow{AC}$ [1]
2. a) Scalar   [1]
   b) Vector   [1]
   c) Vector   [1]

Page 42

1. a) k = 52° (alternate segment)   [1]
   b) l = 90° (angle subtended from
      diameter)   [1]
   c) m = 48° (96° ÷ 2) [1]; n = 42°
      ((180° – 96°) ÷ 2) [1]
2. a) a = radius [1]; b = circumference [1];
      c = arc [1]; d = segment [1];
      e = sector [1]
   b) Arc length $= \frac{\theta}{360} \times 2 \times \pi \times r$ [1];
      Arc length $= \frac{40}{360} \times 2 \times 3.14 \times 10$
      = 6.977 777 778 [1];
      Arc length = 6.98cm [1]

1. $8a + 6b$ [1]
2. a) $\overrightarrow{AC}$ = 4c – 4a   [1]
   b) $\overrightarrow{AP} = \frac{1}{4}(4c - 4a)$ = c – a   [1]
   c) $\overrightarrow{DP}$ = 4a + c – a = 3a + c   [1]
3. a) True   [1]
   b) False   [1]

Graph Paper